Frances Cohen is a 73-year-old widow. She was a 'stay at home mum' to her three children, who have now given her seven, in her words: "handsome, beautiful, adorable, clever and unique grandchildren!" But then every grandma says that don't they? They now age from eighteen down to seven, and over the years she has enjoyed writing special poems for their birthdays, but also teaching them trivia, including some rather bizarre "collective nouns" for various animals and birds.

A PRICKLE OF PORCUPINES - REALLY!

A COLLECTION OF AMUSING AND EDUCATIONAL POEMS
INCLUDING SOME WONDERFUL 'COLLECTIVE NOUNS'

BY FRANCES COHEN

ILLUSTRATED BY HER GRANDCHILDREN: BILLIE AND OZ YELLAND, JACOB AND MYA COHEN

AUSTIN MACAULEY PUBLISHERS™
LONDON · CAMBRIDGE · NEW YORK · SHARJAH

A CIP catalogue record for this title is available from the British Library.

ISBN 9781398468818 (Paperback)
ISBN 9781398468825 (ePub e-book)

www.austinmacauley.com

First Published 2023
Austin Macauley Publishers Ltd®
1 Canada Square
Canary Wharf
London
E14 5AA

Dedicated to all my precious grandchildren.

During the COVID pandemic, Frances decided to combine, the sometimes quirky collective nouns of animals, into poems, which resulted in, A Prickle of Porcupines! Really? Learn more... But as she delved into some rather interesting facts to include in her poems, she also discovered that sometimes, there was more than one word for "the group name". She has tried to include them all but acknowledges that the following may not be comprehensive and some may be from inaccurate sources.

As she discovered, this really is not an "exact science", but nevertheless, a lot of fun! The added touch was to get some of her grandchildren to illustrate the book, and oh, she has made up her own collective noun for her grandchildren.
A DELIGHT!

Alpaca

Alpacas are mammals,
Not llamas or camels.
Their fleece grows thickly
And is soft, not prickly.
It's woven to make blankets and mats
Socks, scarves, foot warmers and also hats.
If they get cross or scared, I have to admit,
They are not so nice, because they will spit!
But lots together is an easy word
Just like with cows, the word is HERD.

B.Y.

Antelope

Antelopes are herbivores and some have stripes,
And, in fact, would you believe,
there are 91 different types.
The smallest is called "royal", but then the
largest is grand,
Because he is called the giant eland.
But whatever their size, colour or weight,
Nearly all have horns; either spiral,
curved or straight.
They have short tails and you can take my word,
If you see lots together, it's called a
DROVE or a HERD.

O.Z

Ants

Apart from Antarctica, ants live in every
other place.
With 12,000 different species, and you should
know this, in case…
you come across a bullet ant because then
you need to watch out,
They really have the most painful sting, there
is no doubt.
Ants have no ears, and some not even eyes,
But they are a source of food to many,
including beetles and flies.
There is one egg-laying queen, female workers,
and the males just mate,
Did you know, they are incredibly strong, they
carry 50 times their own body weight.
They help the world as they turn and aerate
the soil, and it's certainly not barmy,
To know that when they are together,
it's called a SWARM or an ARMY.

Ape

Apes are primates and come in lots of sizes
and shapes.
They are agile and clever and eat plants, leaves
and grapes.
They use their hands and feet to eat and climb,
And love playing with their friends and having
a good time.
But they can also be naughty, and are known
for their rudeness,
And if you see lots together,
it is called a SHREWDNESS!

Baboon

Baboons are primates, and omnivores, and
can be mainly found
During the day hunting for food and playing
on the ground.
They come in different colours; yellow, silver,
brown and green,
And love a daily routine, including grooming
to keep clean.
Their loose cheeks store food for later, and
they have large dog-like muzzles for a nose,
They grunt, scream, smack their lips and have
five fingers and five toes.
They are very sociable and enjoy being with
each other,
And there is a very special bond between each
baby and their mother.
At night time, they will climb trees to sleep in
a small group,
And the special word, when you see them
together, is a TROOP.

Bat

Bats can be red, tan, grey or brown,
And they sleep all day, upside down.
The flying fox is the largest one you can find
They have very small eyes and are almost blind.
At sunset, they wake to find food
during the night,
And use their ears, not eyes, to give them sight.
They eat flies and mosquitoes, and bat
poop is for sure
Quite valuable and useful and used as manure.
Hundreds and thousands live together, it is
quite a crowd,
And this is when they are called a
COLONY or a CLOUD.

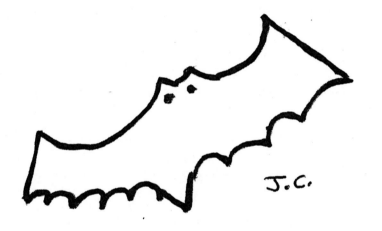

Bear

Bears come in lots of different colours and size.
They have a great sense of smell and hearing,
and very strong eyes.
They mostly walk on all four of their paws,
At the end of which they have very
long claws
Which helps them climb trees where
they like to take a nap,
Also to keep them safe, while they are
having a snack.
They can also stand on their two back legs,
and this is merely,
So they can have a good look around, and see
more clearly.
They eat plants, berries and insects but their
favourite dish
Is definitely a lovely, juicy,
freshly caught fish.
They can make lots of different noises,
though they cannot howl,
But grunting, huffing and certainly a
great big growl.
And if you see lots of them together,
I can tell you the truth,
The collective name for them is a SLEUTH.

B.Y.

Bee

Bees are insects and do amazing work,
From collecting pollen they do not shirk.
Helping plants and fruit to grow,
And honey, of course, did you know…?
They are the only insect that makes food for us,
And they do it all without making a fuss.
In sunny weather, or even in a storm,
if you see lots of them together,
it's called a SWARM.

Bird

There are thousands of different birds
in the world,
And some look quite splendid with their
feathers unfurled.
Like peacocks or swans and even the eagle,
All so magnificent and really quite regal.
But then there are the ones that are
not very tall,
Blue tits, sparrows and robins are
all quite small.
Some float on water or sit on a rock
But when they are all together,
it's called a FLOCK.

A.Y.

Butterfly

Well, it starts with a caterpillar who has
a very short lifespan,
And his only job, while alive,
is to eat as much as he can!
Then he becomes a chrysalis,
and we wait a while,
And what happens next will really
make you smile.
We see the beautiful butterfly, oh,
what a sight!
And if there are lots together,
they are called a FLIGHT.

O.Y.

Camel

I guess they are known for their long
legs and hump,
And you need to know this is more than
just a bump.
It's full of fat which they can live off for
40 plus days.
While living in the desert with all that sand
and sun's rays.
Is no problem for them with three sets of
eyelids, and more,
They can drink 40 gallons of water and
keep it in store.
So in the heat of the desert,
they don't need a fan,
And if you see lots of them together,
it's called a CARAVAN

Cat

Some cats are wild, they are called
feral, and yet...
Most of them today are domestic,
and somebody's pet
They can jump six times their length,
and with much glee,
Can easily climb up any tree.
But because their claws are
downward curved,
This really might sound quite absurd,
At coming down the tree, they are the worst,
And have to do it very slowly, tail-first.
They love cat naps, and to groom their fur,
And when they are happy, they purr and purr.
But when in fear or stress, they hiss
and splutter,
And lots together is a CLOWDER,
POUNCE, or a CLUTTER!

Cheetah

Did you know that Cheetahs are the fastest
animal by far?
They are even faster than the fastest
sports car!
They are carnivores, only eating
meat and...more...
They purr and meow like cats, and do not ROAR!
They prefer to be alone but in addition,
If you do see lots of them,
it's called a COALITION!

Cobra

One of the most venomous of snakes, which
looks particularly grand,
When angry or threatened will make the ribs
in his neck expand.
This makes a hood, which is a
magnificent sight,
But you better watch out, because he can kill
with just one bite.
Within minutes, his victim will be dead, and
then his goal,
Is to swallow his prey, whatever the size,
completely whole.
The king cobra is the largest and longest snake
in the world,
And can measure up to 4 meters long when
he is unfurled.
The snake charmer will play his music to make
them dance,
And it is quite a sight to see, as if the snake
is in a trance.
Seeing one is scary, but lots together would
make anyone shiver,
And then the collective name for them
is a QUIVER.

O.Y.

Crocodile

Did you know the crocodile is the
biggest reptile by far?
And closest to the dinosaurs,
they really are.
Whether on the water or beneath,
They can have up to 100 teeth.
They move real fast so you better
watch out.
If you see one coming, give a big shout!
But remember this, whatever
their location,
If you see lots of them together, it's called
a CONGREGATION!

Dog

Dogs can be large and small, and there are
hundreds of breeds,
And they have the ability to fulfil many of
our needs.
They are forty times better than us when it
comes to sense of smell,
And this helps them do many good things
exceedingly well.
They can round up sheep and
smell out drugs,
And guide the blind and help the police
track thugs.
Some run so fast that they have special
dog races,
And they are used to guard all sorts of
different places.
They can bark and growl and be
a bit snappy,
But they love to wag their tails when they
are feeling happy.
Some entertain us by learning lots of tricks,
And if they want to show love, they give
lots of licks.
They can pull large sledges over any
snowy track,
And if there are lots of them together, it is
called a PACK!

B20

Dolphin

Dolphins are mammals, have great eyesight
and keen ears,
They can dive up to 1,000 feet and live for
up to 50 years.
They have one baby at a time, who drink
milk from their mothers
And they are all very friendly and love to
be with others.
If one is sick, they do their best to care,
And they use their blowholes to get
their fresh air.
If you see lots of them together, the only
thing that is odd,
Is that it can be called a SCHOOL or a POD.

Donkey

Donkeys are clever and stronger
than a horse,
And have excellent memories and
of course,
In countries that have no trucks, and really
bad roads,
They are excellent at carrying people, and
also large loads.
They are incredibly nimble, and in both the
dry and rain,
Can walk for miles on any kind of terrain.
They eat straw and lush grass, but if you
want to give them a treat,
Carrots, turnips, swedes and apples, they
really love to eat.
Their large ears keep them cool, and when
they bray,
Did you know this can be heard up to 60
miles away?

They are very sociable, and really
love to spend,
Time with another donkey, who has become
their best friend.
They are thought to be stubborn,
but this is not true,
They just like to think ahead
about everything they do.
And when gathered together, again there
is more than one word,
They can be called either a
DROVE or a HERD.

Duck

Wild ducks usually lay about 12 eggs,
just once a year
And one thing about this is very clear,
They spend much time making a
really comfy nest,
Lined with lovely soft feathers that they
take from their own breast.
Unlike domestic ducks, who are more
than happy to lay
Throughout the year, at least one
egg every day.
They love the water, and whatever
their mood
Will forage and dive for
all kinds of food.
Plants, small fish and insects are
their usual diet,
And apart from the occasional quack,
they are usually quite quiet.
Their large webbed feet help them waddle,
and on water, they float,
And their amazing feathers give them a
completely waterproof coat.

The males are called drakes, and females
hens, and this might sound quite daft,
But lots together can be called, a TEAM,
BUNCH, FLUSH, a PADDLING or a RAFT.

Eel

There are 800 different types of this
snake-like fish
And in many countries, they are regarded
as a very tasty dish.
In Japan, China and Spain,
they are all very keen
To add this delicacy to their local cuisine.
In 18-century England, though,
in London's East End,
Many of the poor on jellied
eels would depend.
They were cheap, nutritious and
very tasty, I am told,
Taken from the River Thames and then off
to the market to be sold.
Eels like shallow water, and are usually
only active at night,
When they lay in wait for their prey, to give
them a big fright.
They love worms, snails and mussels,
which they love to grab,
And also fish, shrimp and a
lovely juicy crab.
But from an electric eel, you really
need to bolt,
They can really bite you hard with
a 650 volt.

Eels are usually solitary fish, but it has
to be said,
If they do gather together, they are called a
SWARM or a BED.

Elephant

Elephants are the largest animals
who live on the land,
With their thick skin and long trunks,
they are simply grand.
Their tusks are made of ivory,
and did you know,
These tusks get bigger and longer,
and grow and grow?
There are two types of elephant, Indian
and African, and both are smart,
The Africans have the larger ears, that is
how you tell them apart.
They remember things for years and
take my word,
If you see lots together, they can be called
a MEMORY, a PARADE or a HERD.

B.Y.

Fox

Most foxes are red, but some can be grey,
And you don't see them so much during
the hours of day.
They don't gather in groups, but alone
can be found
In the dens that they dig under the ground.
Even though related to dogs, this is a fact,
They have much more in common
with a cat.
They stalk and pounce on their prey, and
with great ease,
They are also able to climb up and down
most trees.
They have sensitive whiskers on their legs
and face,
And when it comes to speed,
they can run apace.
You may see them at night even in the
country or in towns,
And they can amazingly make
40 different sounds.
When it comes to food, they are
not fussy at all,
They will eat what they find, whether
big or small.

They are known to be clever,
and even cunning,
And their tails, called brushes,
are really quite stunning.
Although very unlikely to see them in bulk,
Their collective name is either
LEASH or a SKULK!

Ferret

Ferrets are related to weasels
and polecats,
And one of their many uses is to chase
and kill rats,
To protect the grain that is in barns, and
believe it or not,
They're also used to pull wires through
long thin pipes quite a lot.
They are very popular as pets and
did you know,
They were domesticated over
2,000 years ago?
They are known to be fearless, and
if they get the chance,
They really love to jump and dance.
They are carnivores and their biggest treat,
Is to have a lovely meal of some
fresh raw meat.
There is only one species, but you may
need to note,
They can have up to twenty different
kinds of coat.
Now, if there are lots together, would you
like to guess?
The special word for the ferret is a
BUSYNESS!

B.Y.

Frog

Frogs start as tadpoles, and after
14 weeks have gone by,
The frog is formed, with long back legs
that help him leap high.
On top of his head are his eyes and nose,
And at the end of his feet, he has
extremely long toes.
He has a long sticky tongue, of which
he is very fond,
To find snails, slugs and worms in the
local pond.
He drinks through his skin, which is slimy
and smarmy,
And if you see lots of them together,
it is called an ARMY.

A.Y.

Giraffe

Giraffes are the very tallest animal by far,
With their long legs and necks,
they really are!
They only eat plants, and really love
those high-up leaves,
With their long necks and long tongues,
they can reach with ease.
They are quiet, drink little water, but
have great eyesight,
Which helps a lot when a lion comes near,
wanting to bite!
But watch out, lion, in any direction
they can kick,
And with one of those kicks,
your death can be quick!
They roam in groups, and whatever
the day or hour,
If you see them all together,
it is called a TOWER.

B.Y.

Goose

If you have more than one goose,
the word is geese,
And if you are near them and want some
quiet and peace,
You need to know something and it is this,
They will chase you away with loud
honks and a hiss.
They love to eat berries,
nuts and lots of seeds,
And their other favourite food is lush
grass and weeds.
Many are kept as pets, and they
are cheap to keep
Providing lots of eggs and
some tasty meat.
They fly in a V shape and believe it or not,
They take it in turns to have the lead spot.
Along with the swan they are the
largest waterfowl to be found
But they prefer to spend most of
their time on dry ground,
And then they are called a GAGGLE,
but then again…
When flying in the air, they are
called a SKEIN!

Gorilla

Gorillas are the largest primates
and very smart,
They share 98% of our DNA,
where can I start?
They have hands and feet just like us,
And communicate easily with each other,
without any fuss.
They can also make simple tools, I am told,
And the mums nurse their
babies until three years old.
They never let their infants
out of their sight,
And carry them on their backs,
or hug them tight.
They have quite short legs,
but their arms are long,
And the silverback male is very,
very strong.
They make comfy beds to sleep in
during the night,
And watching them play in the
day is a delight.
They always stay within a family group,
And the name for this is a
BAND or a TROOP!

O.Y.

Hedgehog

The hedgehog is mainly known for
his prickly back,
Which certainly gives protection
when under attack.
Up to 7,000 spines keep them safe
from most,
Apart from badgers and owls, and
then they are toast.
They sleep all day, and are awake all night,
When they roam around looking for
a tasty bite.
Insects, worms, snails and mice,
And they also think
frogs taste quite nice.
During the wintertime, they
take a long rest,
Hibernating in a nice comfy leafy nest.
They are solitary animals,
though I have to say,
When together, they are called a
PRICKLE or an ARRAY!

O.Y,

Hippopotamus

The head and the body of the hippo
are very large,
And on land, despite their short legs,
are very apt to charge,
At any foe they see, they will
chase and attack,
They are aggressive and can kill many
with a mighty thwack.
They spend most of their day
out of the heat, keeping cool,
Standing or floating in a river, lake or pool.
On top of their head are their eyes,
ears and nose,
And when in the water, this is
really all that shows.
In the cool of night, they come out
to graze and feast,
And can eat up to 150 lbs of grass at least.
They love being together, and then there is
not just one word,
They can be called a BLOAT,
a CRASH, or simply a HERD!

B.Y.

Hyena

Hyenas are known as ugly, clever and sly,
The smallest carnivore,
with a very strange cry,
Like a giggle or laugh, and they
are seen as a pest.
But when it comes to hunting,
they really are the best.
With their strong jaws, paws and claws,
they are a winner
Eating bones, horns, hooves and
teeth for their dinner.
They hunt in groups, and are
similar to the jackal,
And when you see them all together,
it is called a CACKLE!

IBIS

The Ibis is known for their long legs and
long curved bill.
They love to wade in groups, but you will
never hear them trill.
They make a sort of grunt, as they look
for a tasty dish,
Crabs, snakes, and frogs, but their
favourite is crayfish.
They love swamps, marshes and lakes,
but make their nest in a tree,
And they come in so many different
colours, just look and see.
They gather in hundreds and thousands in
the water or on the land,
And if you see them all together,
it is called a STAND.

Iguana

The Iguana is actually just considered,
To be one of the very largest of lizards.
They can be blue, orange,
purple and green,
But it is the green that is
most commonly seen.
They adore the sun and like to
find a nice spot,
Where they can just sit and get sticky
and very, very hot.
But if a predator comes while they are
having a snooze,
They will swish their tail to
bewilder and confuse.
And on top of their head, they
have a third "eye"
To spot any predator coming
down from the sky.
They sometimes grow to over six feet,
And plants, fruit and leaves are
what they like to eat.
They also enjoy a swim, and
you will never guess,
That when there are lots together,
it is called a MESS!

B.Y.

Jellyfish

Jellyfish have been around for
millions of years,
They are 95% water and have no brains,
bones, or ears.
Even though they have long tentacles,
they are not very smart,
They also have no eyes and
not even a heart.
150 million people get stung by
them every year,
So they are not very popular when
near your beach they appear.
So if you see them coming,
you better draw back,
And if there are lots of them together,
it is called a SMACK!

Kangaroo

Kangaroos are marsupials and
eat mainly grass,
And at hopping on their large back legs,
they are really first class.
They have a large tail and come in two
colours, either red or grey,
They either grunt or cough, but never bray!
On four legs, however,
they walk very slowly,
And did you know their babies are
called a Joey?
They move quickly on land, and also at
swimming they do a good job,
And if you see lots all together,
it is called a MOB.

Koala

Koalas are marsupials, not bears,
and can be found
In Eucalyptus trees and rarely
on the ground.
This is where they eat leaves and
sleep all night long,
And if you think they need water,
you would be wrong.
The Eucalyptus leaf gives them
all they need
And it is on these leaves only
that they feed.
Up to a kilo a day, even though to most,
These leaves are poisonous, and
if eaten, you'll be toast!
When born, the babies in their
mum's pouch will stay,
For up to six months, all night and all day.
The only time Koalas need to watch out
Is if there are owls or dingoes about.
So even though the tree is
their usual location,
If you do see lots together,
it is called a POPULATION!

Leopard

The Leopard is fierce, fast,
ferocious and scary,
He can leap and climb, and his
prey should be wary.
He prowls at night to find something
tasty to eat,
Using stealth and patience to find
some nice fresh meat.
Whether antelope, deer or monkey,
with one bite
To their neck, he will give, so they have
no chance to fight.
He is extremely strong and sometimes
will take his prey
Up into a tree, whatever it may weigh.
He has distinctive spots on his
yellow goldish fur,
And when he is content,
he gives a loud purr.
But during the day, he will climb a tree
and choose
A nice comfy branch to have a long snooze.
Even though they are solitary,
when awake or asleep,
If you do see lots together,
it is called a LEAP.

Lion

Lions are called the king of the jungle,
and what's more...
Out of all the big cats, they have
the loudest roar!
They usually go out hunting at night
for their lunch,
And this is done by the females, though
everyone gets to have a munch.
There is a magnificent mane around
the neck of all the males
And they also have a tuft at
the end of their tails.
Now if you see lots of them together,
you had better hide,
And then the special name for
them is a PRIDE.

O.Y.

Mice

They are rodents, quite small, and
one is called a mouse.
With a long tail and pointed, nose, no one
wants them in their house.
They are grey and can crawl through
the tiniest gap,
So many try to stop them from entering
by laying a trap.
They can jump, climb, swim and
their hearing is swell,
Their eyesight is poor but they have
a fantastic sense of smell.
Their teeth never stop growing, so
best not to give them a cuddle,
And if you see lots of them together,
it is called a MUDDLE.

Mole

Moles are very active all year 'round,
Though of course this is all done
under the ground.
With their curved front paws and a
squeak and a wheeze,
In an hour, they can dig up to
18 ft. with ease.
Their sight is not good, so things are a blur,
Because their tiny eyes are covered in fur.
But their long pink snout makes up for this,
And there are not many worms
that they will miss.
They stun them with a toxin and
keep them in a stack
In a larder underground, so a meal
they never lack.
There are many gardeners who
see moles as a pest.
When the molehills appear on their lawns,
they get quite stressed.
But even though nice lawns
they seem to spoil,
Their constant digging under-ground
actually aerates the soil.

Moles are solitary, so I am not
sure from whence,
Collectively the names LABOUR
or COMPANY really make no sense.

Monkey

There are 264 different species of
monkeys in all
The Mandrill the largest, and the
Capuchin very small.
Some live up in the trees, but then
others are found
Nearly all of their days upon the ground.
They bark, scream, squeak,
chatter and growl,
But guess what, the Howler
Monkeys actually howl!
They mostly eat fruit, leaves and nuts,
but for a treat,
The Mandrill will happily kill to
get some meat.
In 1948, the US put a monkey in a rocket,
do you know why?
This rhesus monkey called Albert was
sent high in the sky
To see if he would survive,
seemed quite a long shot,
And sadly, survive poor Albert did not.
But then again, if you see monkeys
in a large group
This can be called TRIBE,
MISSION or a TROOP.

J.C.

Nightingale

The Nightingale is best known for
its beautiful song,
But did you know they are in West Africa
all winter long?
Then they return in time
for the spring,
And it is just the males who once
again will sing.
They return to breed and then their
nests can be found
Not up in the trees, but just
above ground.
Now here is something I am sure you
did not know,
Cellist Beatrice Harrison did a
live radio show
Way back in 1924, she
played along
With the Nightingale as he sang his song.
Now if you do see lots of
them gathered together,
The word is WATCH,
whatever the weather.

Otter

Otters love swimming and they
are pretty speedy,
And when it comes to eating, they are
also quite greedy.
They love to fish, but they also do really well
In using a rock to crack a clams shell.
The babies are born in the water but their
mums are aware
That they cannot swim for a month, so
they have to take care.
They use abandoned beavers lodges,
which helps them shirk,
Giving them a comfy nest without
any of the work.
They all love to play, and it is
certainly a delight,
Seeing them make a slide, it's quite a sight.
In Bangladesh, otters are used to lure the
fish into the net,
So the fishermen there think they
are a great asset.
Strangely, when they poop,
apparently the smell
Is more like violets, now isn't that swell?
So if you see lots together, in a river,
lake or swamp,
They are called a BEVY, RAFT,
LODGE or even a ROMP.

Owl

Owls are probably known for their
flat faces and huge eyes,
And not everyone knows that they
have many different cries.
They can screech, hiss, whinny and of
course, twit twoo
And the saw-whet owl sounds
like a saw, it's true!
They can also vary in colour and size,
And did you know they cannot
move their eyes?
But that is okay, because
with great ease
They can turn their heads a
whole 270 degrees.
They have excellent hearing
and extremely good sight,
And are completely silent when
they are in flight.
They are lazy and prefer to use
other birds' nests,
And farmers love them, cos they
eat all the pests.
The smallest is the Elf Owl, and
the largest is the Great Grey,
But you will very seldom see any
of them during the day.

At night, they are out hunting
with great intent,
And when there are lots together,
it is called a PARLIAMENT.

Ostrich

The Ostrich is the largest bird,
But they cannot fly, which seems absurd.
However, with their long legs
and the powerful thigh,
They can run faster than most
birds can fly.
Up to 70km per hour they
are able to achieve.
Covering five meters with one stride,
would you believe?
They have very large eyes, which
gives great assistance,
To being able to see far into the distance.
If predators get too close,
it will just take one kick,
Whether lion or cheetah,
their death will be quick.
It's said that they bury their heads
in the sand, I don't know why,
Because it's just not true, in
fact, a complete lie.
So if you do happen to see a lot of
them outside,
This can be called a FLOCK,
WOBBLE or a PRIDE.

Giant Panda

The giant panda is a large bear, that is
black and white,
Not to be confused with the Red Panda,
that is...well, red and quite slight.
The wild ones live in China, in
forests full of bamboo,
And guess what? This is mainly
on what they chew.
They will eat for up to 16 hours, and
I also have to say,
They usually do a "poop" 40 times
every day!
Along with their sharp teeth, and an
extended wrist bone, like a
thumb, I am told,
They are well able to grab bamboo shoots
and then keep a very firm hold.
Their babies are born quite helpless, they
are blind and really small,
And it takes many, many months before
they can stand or even crawl.
The males will often do a hand-stand up
against a tree,
To mark their territory with a great big wee!
They are actually quite solitary,
but in the unlikely event
You see lots together, it's a
BAMBOO or EMBARRASSMENT.

Pelican

The family of the pelican is over 30
million years old,
From fossils found in France,
so I am assuredly told.
Their bills are huge, and underneath
you can hardly ignore,
The large fibrous pouch that dangles,
but this is not for food to store.
It's actually very useful,
like a net to catch the fish
Which they will eat at once,
a very tasty dish.
When it comes to building a nest, neither
male nor female shirk,
They both pull their weight and
it's perfect teamwork.
Once the eggs are laid, they will stand
on them, not sit,
And once again this work between
males and females is split.
The brown and Peruvian pelican have
an amazingly keen eye,
Being able to spot a fish underwater
while flying high in the sky.

The white pelican has a yellow horn and
this will only appear
During the mating season for three
months every year.
And when they all gather together, you
might think it a little odd,
You can then call them a POUCH, BRIEF,
SCOOP or a POD.

Penguin

Penguins are birds, with no wings,
and can't fly
But instead, they have flippers,
do you know why?
So they can hunt for fish when
they swim in the sea
And you wouldn't believe how
fast they can be.
But then on the land, they can waddle,
run or hop,
Or slide on the ice, when on their
bellies they flop!
They will huddle in thousands to keep
themselves warm
From the biting cold winds or
even a snowstorm.
They all live in the southern hemisphere
and the largest of all
Is the emperor penguin who can be
up to five feet tall.
Once a year, they lose all their feathers,
and they have a long sharp beak,
And the call they make to each other is
completely unique.
The collective word is RAFT when you see
them swimming together,

But then when on the land,
whatever the weather,
When they gather together to have a
nice big cuddle,
They can be called a ROOKERY, COLONY,
WADDLE or a HUDDLE.

A.Y.

Pig

Pigs were domesticated over
6,000 years ago,
First in China, but there are many
other things to know.
They are actually very clean and
extremely clever,
Have an amazing sense of smell, and do
they sweat? Actually never!
So to say someone "sweats like a pig"
is simply not true,
They have no sweat glands, and so this is
something they cannot do!
They can learn their own names and tricks,
faster than a dog,
The female is called a sow and the
male boar or hog.
They prefer the cold so when it is too hot,
They will cool themselves by wallowing in
a lovely muddy spot.
They can run really fast and
they grunt and squeal,
And will eat anything they find for a
nice tasty meal.
They are extremely friendly
and very chummy,
And love a good scratch on their back
or their tummy.

Now when they are all together, you can
choose from many a word,
FLOCK, PARCEL, DROVE, SOUNDER,
DRIFT or a HERD.

O.Y.

Quail

Quails are game birds, and they are
very closely related
To pheasants, and both their meat and
flesh are highly rated.
They have portly bodies, and their plumage
is unique,
Some have a head plume and all a curved
and small beak.
Their predators are many both
animal and fowl,
Including cats, foxes, hawks and
also the owl.
Their high-pitched cackle and grunt can
be quite loud,
And they love to have a bath in a
large dust cloud.
They are mainly solitary, though can be
seen in a pair,
And spend most of their time on the
ground, not in the air.

So when you do see lots together, there is
a special reason,
It is a sign that it is their annual
mating season.
And then when you see them in
this large block,
This can be called a COVEY, BEVY or
simply a FLOCK.

Rabbit

Rabbits have large ears, which they can
turn with ease,
In fact, up to one hundred and
eighty degrees!
With excellent hearing, plus keen
eyes to see,
They are always ready from their
predators, to flee.
They do a zig-zag run and are off
at the double,
And this helps them to usually keep
out of trouble.
They eat their own 'poo' and it also
worth knowing
That their teeth actually, never
stop growing.
They have a special "binky" leap which is
really quite quirky,
Which they love to do when they are feeling
happy and chirpy.
They came over to England with the
Norman conquest,
Who used their fur and their meat, they
loved the best.
To "breed like rabbits" is a saying
that is true,
Because they have lots and lots of babies,
they really do.

One of the collective names is WARREN,
but here is a list of the rest,
HERD, FLOCK, COLONY, FLICK,
DROVE or a NEST.

Rat

Rats are rodents, and seem to
manage to survive,
Wherever they are, they
increase and thrive.
Living amongst rubbish and sewers
I have to admit,
To humans, deadly diseases
they can transmit.
Their eyes are quite weak, but they have a
great sense of smell, And at
memorising a route, they really excel.
Their extremely sharp teeth can chew
through wire and more,
Also glass, brick, wood and lead,
for them is no chore.
They originated in Asia, but then when
ships' sails were unfurled,
They were carried to every single country
in the world.
Strangely in some countries, it is
seen as a great treat,
Like China and Thailand, they actually
eat rat meat!
The most famous rat catcher was a
dog called "Hatch"
Who sailed on the Mary Rose, and

many a rat did catch.
When it comes to a collective name, for
choice we do not lack,
PLAGUE, RABBLE, COLONY, SWARM,
HORDE, MISCHIEF or a PACK.

Rhinoceros

Rhinos are huge, and you might
like to know,
They appeared on earth over 50 million
years ago.
Back then, they were woolly,
and then they became,
Well, less woolly, but otherwise
exactly the same.
Their horns can grow very long,
and are not bone or skin,
But a special protein that is called keratin.
And this protein is exactly the same kind
That in human hair and nails you will find.
The largest rhino up to
3,500 kilos can weigh,
And both black and white rhinos
are actually grey.
They are plant eaters, and even
though they are vast,
They can actually run extremely fast.
So if you see lots of them together, you
really need to dash,
Then the word for them can
be STUBBORNNESS, HERD
or a CRASH.

A.Y.

Reindeer

The Reindeer, of course, is a
species of deer,
And survive in snow, for 40% of the year
In the Arctic, Alaska, Greenland and
Russia too,
But the ones in North America
are called Caribou
The Inuit hunt them for their antlers,
fur and meat,
But other predators think their baby
calves are a treat.
So if a golden eagle is hovering,
they better beware,
But also watch out for a wolf or a bear.
There are two things about them which
are quite strange
In the summer and winter, both their
eyes and hooves change To adapt
to the seasonal light and ground
And the collective name is HERD if
lots of them are found.

M.C.

Snail

Over 60,000 species of snails can be found
Both in the sea and ocean and
on the ground
They are actually just slugs with
an added shell
And have two sets of feelers that help them
see and smell.
They lay up to 80 eggs, and newborn snails,
even though small,
Come out of the egg with shell and all.
On the ground, they move
incredibly slow,
About 2 cm. a second is the
fastest they go.
But if they are in danger they are
incredibly slick
At retreating into their shell,
slickety quick.
If you think they are all small,
you would be wrong,
The Giant African Snail can be
over 30 cm. long.
Now in France, you may already know
They eat the snails that they call, escargot.
And the collective word, is really great fun,
It is a WALK of snails, certainly not a run!!!

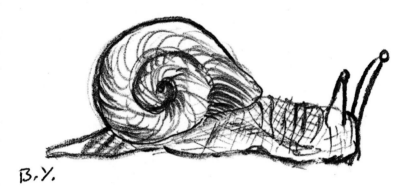

B.Y.

Squirrel

There are 200 species of Squirrels, but
types only three,
Ground Squirrels, Flying Squirrels, and
then, well "Tree"
They are fast and nimble and if
they need to dash,
With a twitch of the tail, they are
gone in a flash.
Their tails are amazing, and
really quite cute,
And when leaping, give balance,
and act as a parachute.
They eat nuts, seeds, insects,
and what more...
The acorns they bury, to keep
them in store.
Because of the way their eyes are aligned,
They can actually see both
front and behind.
They build nests, called dreys, for two
reasons, I'm told,
To give birth to their babies, and to keep
warm when it's cold.
There are squirrels the world over, but it is
really just the Grey
That you are most likely to see
here in the UK.

Whether in Yorkshire, Derbyshire or
even in Surrey,
The collective name for them
is SCURRY..

A.Y.

Tiger

The Tiger is by far the largest wild cat
And no two have the same stripes,
that is a fact.
The Siberian is the largest,
but the most well-known,
Is the Bengal Tiger,
and they mostly, all live alone.
They just eat meat, and have a
huge appetite,
So after sleeping all day,
they then go hunting at night.
They are patient and quiet as
they stalk their prey
Then quick as a flash, their victim,
they will slay.
They can all run at an incredible speed,
Up to 65 mph, they can easily exceed.
They make lots of different noises,
and some examples of this,
Are a grunt, growl, moan, snarl,
roar or even a hiss.
I am sure you have never seen any
in your home town,
But an AMBUSH of tigers is the
collective noun.

A.Y.

Turtle

There are seven types of turtles that live in
the sea and on land,
And they all lay their eggs buried
deep in the sand.
As soon as the babies hatch
it is a sight to see,
As they scurry off to the water as
fast as can be.
They are cold-blooded reptiles,
and so I am told,
They can live to become incredibly old.
They mainly feed underwater
and without any fuss,
Can hold their breath for up
to five hours plus.
They are mainly herbivores, but the
Leatherback's favourite dish
Is a juicy, fresh wriggly tasty jellyfish!
On their backs is cartilage,
it is actually not a shell,
Made up of bones, spine and rib cage, that
protect them very well.
Though mainly solitary, in the breeding
season when you see both male and female
Then their special collective noun is BALE

Vulture

Vultures are one of the largest birds
of prey,
But when it comes to feeding,
they seldom slay.
Preferring to eat meat that has been
dead a while,
Carrion, decaying flesh, it all
sounds so vile!
Most have no feathers on their
neck or head
Which helps them keep clean and
infections not to spread.
They have weak legs and feet,
and their talons are blunt.,
But a powerful hooked bill, and they
can also grunt.
They are sociable and like being together,
And then it depends what they are
doing.....whether
When flying, called a KETTLE, but
this is quite witty,
A WAKE when eating together, and
a VENUE or COMMITTEE.

Whale

So the whale that is the biggest mammal in
the whole world, is the Blue,
It weighs the same as twenty-four
elephants, this is absolutely true!
Now the Gray Whale has no teeth, but a
more important fact I must make clear,
He makes the longest migration of any
mammal, up to 22,000 km. every year
The Beluga Whale has a flexible neck, and
makes lots of sounds with great glee,
They can, click, chirp and whistle, and are
called the Canaries of the Sea.
The Narwhale has only two teeth, and one
grows outside like a large prong,
Which they use to stun and spear their
prey, and can be up to 3 meters long.
The smallest is the Minke Whale, and the
Humpback known for his song,
The Killer Whale, eats other whales, and the
Bowhead lives really long.
They mostly have one baby calf
who is always born tail first,
And after birth, for many months, with
their mother's milk are nursed.
Now again, when they are gathered together

there is more than one word,
Usually POD, but also, SCHOOL,
GAME, or HERD.

Zebra

Zebras belong to the family of the horse,
Famous for their black and white
stripes, of course
South and East Africa is their natural home
Where they can be found, and
where they freely roam.
Grazing all day, but then,
if they come under attack,
They all surround the predator, then one,
with a kick, gives a mighty Whack!
Their stripes are unique, if you
carefully look at one,
Trying to find another exactly the same,
you will find none.
Of course, a Zebra Crossing is where you
can safely cross the road,
As long you also remember to follow the
Green Cross Code.
Zebras migrate in very large groups, and
again, there is more than one word
Their collective noun can be ZEAL,
DAZZLE, or just plain HERD.

B.Y.